Anything Is Possible

Books by Keith N. Ferreira

The Intellectual Rebel
Aphorisms
Speculative Aphorisms
Speculative Aphorisms II
Philoscience
Philoscience II
Intellectual Jazz
Intellectual Jazz II
Jazzism
Neoliberal Arts
Neoliberal Arts II
Postmodern Minimalist Philosophy
Simpletism
Uncertaintyism
The Ultimate Truth
Anything Is Possible

Please visit my Web site at: Philophysics.com. Thank you!

Anything Is Possible

Keith N. Ferreira

iUniverse, Inc.
New York Lincoln Shanghai

Anything Is Possible

iUniverse books may be ordered through booksellers or by contacting:

iUniverse
2021 Pine Lake Road, Suite 100
Lincoln, NE 68512
www.iuniverse.com
1-800-Authors (1-800-288-4677)

ISBN-13: 978-0-595-36585-2 (pbk)
ISBN-13: 978-0-595-81016-1 (ebk)
ISBN-10: 0-595-36585-X (pbk)
ISBN-10: 0-595-81016-0 (ebk)

Printed in the United States of America

To My Brother-in-Law,
Dwight Roberts

Contents

Part One

Anything Is Possible

According to the philosophy of uncertaintyism, anything is possible, because nothing is absolutely certain, due to the nature of reality and the law of uncertainty, which states that uncertainty is the only certainty.

I Write Books

I write books because I believe that future generations of humans will appreciate my books much more than present generations do, due to the fact that the struggle between entropy and antientropy cannot be rushed, since it has its own timetable.

People Can Understand

People can understand why anything is possible in this universe by considering the possibility that our universe could be the mind of a desktop nonclassical computer, and no one knows where the desktop nonclassical computer might be located and who or what might be operating the desktop nonclassical computer.

Desktop Nonclassical Computers

Desktop nonclassical computers will be nonadvanced and advanced techno-synergic computers.

It Is Not Debatable

It is not debatable that the Republican Party helps the rich, but it is highly debatable who the Democratic Party really helps. The Democratic Party is sinking fast. More power to the Republican Party!

A Superpower in Forty Years

In 1975, I told Israel that they could become a superpower someday, and now I know for sure that Israel can become a superpower within the next 40 years, if they were to develop advanced technosynergic computers during the next 40 years. I am helping the U.S. and Israeli governments, because most other people of the world are too stupid to benefit from my knowledge.

Will Make Obsolete

Advanced technosynergic computers will make all other military weapon systems obsolete in the next 40 years or so.

I Deliberately

In 1972, I deliberately told government scientists to give my Ph.D.s to the Congress so that I could observe how people would react to me over the years. Everyone reacted to me the way one would react to someone who did not have advanced academic degrees, although I spoke or wrote to them the same way that I would have spoken or written to them if they knew that I had advanced academic degrees.

Punitive and Humiliating

The Democratic Party is famous for enacting punitive and humiliating laws for the general public to obey. The Democratic Party is sinking fast. More power to the Republican Party!

The Universe and Beyond

In 1972, I told Congress that I had plans for them. Well, the plans that I had for the Congress was for the U.S. to conquer the universe and beyond, and the Congress is on track to do just that.

Academic Brilliance

People who are fascinated by academic brilliance should always remember the saying, "All that glitters is not gold," because academic brilliance usually represents fool's gold.

The Panuniversal Panaceas

Advanced technosynergic computers will be the panuniversal panaceas that the alchemists were seeking all along, because advanced technosynergic computers will be able to do anything that it is possible to do in the universe and beyond.

Alchemy

Alchemy will triumph in the end, because advanced technosynergic computers will be the fulfillment of the ultimate dream of the alchemists, which was to create the panuniversal panaceas for the problems of humanity.

Owning Web Sites Instead

Instead of giving money to charities, people should consider owning Web sites instead, because in that way they can better get their ideas across to the Internet community, and in doing so, their money will be much better spent as well.

Sir Isaac Newton

Apparently, Sir Isaac Newton thought more deeply about gravity than Einstein did, because gravity has to be an instantaneous force, due to the fact that, if gravity was not an instantaneous force, then the gravitational fields of light would have no meaning, since gravity has to travel faster than the velocity of light in a vacuum in order for the gravitational fields of light to have any meaning.

My Charitable Contributions

I consider my published books and my Web site to be my charitable contributions to humanity and all life on our planet.

Inertial Forces

Physicists do not seem to realize that inertial forces can counteract mutual gravitational forces. Therefore, the universe does not have to be expanding or contracting as physicists believe.

Less Than One Idea Each

Some thousand-page modern philosophy books have less than one idea each in them.

Charitable Work

I consider the writings that I do for my free Web site to be charitable work, and I am proud of it. Everyone who writes for free Web sites should consider their writings to be charitable work, and they should be proud of that fact.

Keep Their Asses on Deck

In 1972, I told Congress to keep their asses on deck, to go gently on the control rods, to keep the ship of state on an even keel, and to navigate the ship of state very carefully.

Objective Reality

Objective reality is an unproven and an unprovable hypothesis, because all that anyone can ever perceive are the characteristics of one's own mind. Therefore, everyone is stuck with solipsism forever, whether we like it or not.

Neanderthals and Chimps

Politicians who don't have respect for military veterans are Neanderthals, while non-politicians who don't have respect for military veterans are chimps.

Curved Spacetime

Curved spacetime would cause the paths of matter and energy to curve, but it would not produce the effects of acceleration, because, to matter and energy, curved spacetime would appear uncurved.

Do Not Seem to Realize

What most scientists do not seem to realize is that mathematics can prove anything to be true or false.

I Don't Really Care

I don't really care which people or race win the race to conquer the universe and beyond, because, in the final analysis, it will really be the black race that has won, since all human beings are the descendents of black Africans who lived tens of thousands of years ago.

For National Security Reasons

For national security reasons, the U.S. Congress should abandon their locations in Washington, D.C. and relocate to secure locations in their respective home states as soon as it becomes feasible to do so, because postmodern means of communication make it unnecessary for the U.S. Congress to meet in one location. The U.S. Congress is the most vital part of the U.S. government, because if the U.S. Congress were to be wiped out, it would have serious consequences for the whole world.

The Democratic Party

The Democratic Party tried to neutralize my ass for decades, because I was, and still am the Ultimate Weapon, but now the Republican Party is in full control of the federal government. The Democratic Party is sinking fast. More power to the Republican Party!

If the U.S.

If the U.S. has to compromise on its principles in order to have friends in the rest of the world, then I say, "To hell with the rest of the world, because who needs friends like that." In 1972, I told the Democrats in Congress to fuck the professors, but they did not listen to me. They are still listening to the professors.

Although I Am Not Religious

Although I am not religious, I think that the Democratic Party would be much better off listening to the black Baptist preachers than to the liberal professors, because the liberal professors are dangerous.

High Standards of Bullshit

Liberal professors believe in maintaining high standards of bullshit in academia, but I believe that everyone should be given opportunities to contribute to the academic bullshit.

The Student E. coli

Let's face facts, if something is part of academic knowledge, then it is already outdated. Therefore, academia really consists of sewage processing plants. So why should politicians listen to academics? Students in academia are really academic E. coli, because they are the ones who have to process the bullshit that is fed to them by their teachers and professors. Sewage processing plants do not discriminate, so why should academic sewage processing plants discriminate? Bullshit is bullshit, and all bullshit should be treated equally. Therefore, I say let the student E. coli process all bullshit equally.

Juvenile-monkey Behavior

People might have noticed that I have seldom mentioned the U.S. media in any of my previous books, and that is because I seldom spend time thinking about juvenile-monkey behavior.

Religion

Religion should be taught in public schools, because why should academia discriminate against certain types of bullshit? After all, bullshit is bullshit, and all bullshit should be treated equally. Therefore, I say, religion should be taught in public schools.

Crime

Crime should not be allowed in society, because there is a fundamental conflict between the bullshit of the law and the bullshit of crime.

Bullshitism

Bullshitism is the philosophical doctrine that states that everything is bullshit. Bullshitism is very deep philosophy, because it can solve any problem amicably.

Speech Pattern Changes

It is possible to tell if someone has read a lot of books by their speech pattern. The greater the number of books that the person has read, the greater the changes in their speech pattern will be. The speech pattern changes can increase with the increase in the number of books read, but they cannot decrease, because the speech pattern changes are irreversible.

Academics

What makes academics think that their bullshit is better than other people's bullshit?

Bullshitists

Bullshitists believe that academia should not discriminate against other people's bullshit, because anything is possible in this universe, due to the nature of reality.

I Consider Myself

I consider myself to be a bullshitist, and the founder of the philosophy of bullshitism, which states that everything is bullshit, and that academia should not discriminate against other people's bullshit, because anything is possible in this universe, due to the nature of reality.

If Being Happy

If being happy is so great, then why do some people cry when they feel happy?

The Universe

The universe might be as insignificant as a mouse or a cockroach, so what makes academics think that they are so high and mighty?

Elitist Thieves

The Democratic Party believes in funding and supporting elitist thieves. The Democratic Party is sinking fast. More power to the Republican Party!

It Is Impossible

It is impossible to fuck from a higher position than from the position of humility.

To Women

To women who want to be equal to men, and who want men to open the door for them too, I say, bullshit!

Abortion

Abortion should be banned, because it is murder.

Academic Fascists

Academic fascists value academic proficiency much more highly than creativity and originality. The Democratic Party is sinking fast. More power to the Republican Party!

People Who Don't

People who don't treat the ass with respect are going to rot in hell.

Smarter

Smarter is not always smarter.

If Religious People

If religious people think that the world is coming to an end, then why do they still have children?

The World Democratic Revolution

Fascism is no longer original, but the world democratic revolution is original. The Democratic Party is sinking fast. More Power to the Republican Party!

I Waited

I waited for more than 30 years for a U.S. President to state that the U.S. is engaged in a world democratic revolution. The Republican Party is my dream come true. Congratulations to the Republican Party!

Equal Justice for All

Equal justice for all is as important as American hegemony of the world, the universe, and beyond.

Academics Around the World

Academics around the world ignore genius in their students at their nations' and the world's peril.

The American People

The American People are destined to become sovereign over the world, the universe, and beyond, while the elected politicians in the Republican Party are destined to become the political servants of the American people. The Democratic Party is sinking fast. More power to the Republican Party!

Deserving Academic Degrees

Deserving academic degrees should be more important than earning academic degrees, because earning academic degrees sounds to me more like doing mandatory prison time and getting rewarded for good behavior, while deserving academic degrees means making important contributions to the advancement of knowledge.

I Want to Be Green

I want to be green, because I want to kiss a queen.

Academic Correctional Institutions

Academic correctional institutions are where students go to in order to do academic prison time so that they can be rewarded for good behavior and be punished for bad behavior.

President Bush

President Bush: May the Source be with you!

Senator Bill Frist

Senator Bill Frist: May the Source be with you, too!

Congressman Dennis Hastert

Congressman Dennis Hastert: May the Source be with you also!

Earning vs. Deserving

Earning academic degrees is a form of doing mandatory prison time and being rewarded for good behavior, while deserving academic degrees is a form of meritorious treatment.

To Do Time

To earn something is to do time to get something, while to deserve something is to merit something.

Mathematical Magnitudes

Mathematical magnitudes can either be negative or positive, because the magnitude of a negative area is a negative number, while the magnitude of a positive area is a positive number.

Negative Areas

Negative areas are not impossible as mathematicians believe, because they are facts of mathematics.

Academics Have Known

Academics have known for decades that most geniuses have a hard time coping with academic coping skills, but they have done nothing to remedy the situation, so most geniuses rot without being discovered or being successful at their special talents. The Democratic Party is sinking fast. More power to the Republican Party!

Believe in Carrying Out

The Democratic Party and liberals, in general, believe in carrying out scientific experiments on unsuspecting and vulnerable people in the U.S. and around the world. The Democratic Party is sinking fast. More power to the Republican Party!

Psychological and Psychiatric Torture

The Democratic Party and liberals, in general, believe in carrying out psychological and psychiatric torture on psychiatric patients who they think might be a threat to the status quo. The Democratic Party is sinking fast. More power to the Republican Party!

I Throw My Support

I throw my support to the Republican Party. May the Source be with the Republican Party! The Democratic Party is sinking fast. More power to the Republican Party!

Highly Underestimated

President Bush is highly underestimated, because he is brilliant and genuine gold. May the Source be with President Bush!

If Gravity

If gravity is an instantaneous force as I believe it to be, then virtual and exchange particles would become crap, because the total number of virtual and exchange particles that would exist at any instant of time would make the gravitational fields experienced in the universe much greater than are actually experienced in the universe. Therefore, virtual and exchange particles are unlikely to exist.

A Tuned Antenna

How does a tuned antenna know that it is tuned?

Most Academics

Most academics resent the fact that Dr. Benjamin Franklin did not earn his Ph.D., but that he got his Ph.D., because he deserved it. What most people do not know is that most academics hate people like Dr. Franklin, because people like Dr. Franklin are worth about ten thousand professors.

People Like Dr. Benjamin Franklin

People like Dr. Benjamin Franklin should not have to earn their Ph.D.s, because they deserve their Ph.D.s.

The Right Expression

The right expression is not, "May the Force be with you!" but the right expression is, "May the Source be with you!" because the Source is the cause of the Force, and not vice versa. May the Source be with you!

A Great Captain

President Bush is a great captain. May the Source be with President Bush!

The Only Hope

The only hope for oppressed people around the world is for them to master Western culture, and then try and supersede it, because there are no non-Western ways to out-West the West. May the Source be with you!

Pay No Mind

President Bush: Pay no mind to your critics, because most of them are Lilliputians. You are doing a great job, and I am very proud of you. You saved the country from being ruined by the Democratic Party and liberals, in general.

Rated Pi

President Bush: You are rated pi for political leadership, political martial arts, and I believed that you have also studied some Neoliberal Arts. Congratulations!

Exploring the Universe

If exploring the universe is not important, then what makes anything on the earth important?

The Holy See

The Holy See means the one who sees for the ass, because the ass is holy.

A Papal Bull

A Papal Bull means a Papa bull, or a Papa fuck in the ass.

Dickinson

Dickinson means dick in son.

To Bullshit

To bullshit means to fuck shit.

I Do Not Blame

I do not blame African cannibals, because most Africans are only good to use as food for cannibals.

The Democratic Party's Holy See

The leader of the Democratic Party is the Democratic Party's Holy See, because he or she sees for the Democratic Party's ass, since the Democratic Party's ass is holy.

The Holy Grail

The Holy Grail means the Grail for the ass, because the ass is holy, therefore, the Holy Grail is really the Phallus symbol, since the Cup belongs to whoever claims the Phallus symbol.

The Cup

The Cup goes to the person who claims the Phallus symbol.

God Is a Buller

Folks, God is a buller. In other words, God is a bullshitter.

The One Who Claims

The one who claims the Phallus symbol is the one who fucks the ass, because the ass is holy.

People Are Facing

People are facing their ancestors, because their ancestors are anterior to them, while posterity is posterior to them. In other words, people are fucking their ancestors, and posterity will fuck them in turn.

God

God is anterior and posterior to us. Therefore, we are fucking God, and God will in turn fuck us.

VA Dermatologists

VA dermatologist were checking my scalp for psoriasis about 10 years before the symptoms first appeared.

Carrying Out Experiments

The VA has been carrying out experiments on me for more than 30 years.

One Hundred Percent

President Bush: I support you one hundred percent.

Whatever You Decide to Do

President Bush: Whatever you decide to do, I support you one hundred percent.

An Anal Implant

I believe that the VA gave me an anal implant about three years ago that simulates the symptoms of hemorrhoids.

Fraudulent Diagnosis

I believe that my diagnosis of diabetes is fraudulent. The VA can make fraudulent diagnoses on certain veterans, if they target the veterans for medical research.

Democrats and Liberals

Democrats and liberals, in general, are wonderful people, aren't they?

People Should Be Aware

People should be aware that medical doctors sometimes make fraudulent diagnoses on certain people in order to carry out medical research on them.

You Are Free to Change the Rules

Senator Bill Frist and Congressman Dennis Hastert: You are free to change the rules of the Senate and the House, respectively, as you may see fit to do so. Perhaps, the Democratic Party isn't worth saving after all.

The Word Patient

I do not like the word patient, because it implies that the patient is somehow inferior to the doctor, and the word doctor implies that the doctor is somehow superior to the patient. Doctors are dangerous. Anyone who has the word doctor in front of their name is dangerous.

The Word Doctor

The word doctor is a very dangerous word.

An Example of Naive Common Sense

An example of naive common sense is the belief that the sun rises in the East and sets in the West.

An Example of Nonnaive Common Sense

An example of nonnaive common sense is the belief that the earth spins on its axis and that causes the sun to appear to rise in the East and set in the West.

Help Out Your Fellow Geniuses

President Bush: Help out your fellow geniuses. Please try and help as many of them as you can. Don't forget that the Source is with you.

Traitors

The Democratic Party is made up of traitors, because they were building up Europe so that Europe could rival the U.S.A.

Part Two

The Fundamental Constants

The fundamental constants of the universe were probably designed to be what they are, because the universe might not be fundamental in any sense whatsoever. Nature is probably more than just our universe, because our universe might be as insignificant as a mouse or a cockroach in the larger scheme of things.

Electronic Tags on Terrorists

Electronic tags should be placed on suspected terrorists, and then the suspected terrorists should be released, so that they can be tracked electronically back to their terrorists cells, and, in that way, the terrorists cells can be captured or eliminated.

I Am Helping

I am helping the black race, because the human race is the black race.

Adversity

Adversity can be very intellectually stimulating for the human brain.

Advising All Geniuses

Advising all geniuses: Throw your full support to the Republican Party.

Is More Concerned About

The Democratic Party is more concerned about the mistreatment of suspected terrorists and war detainees than they are about the victims of scientific experimentation or the oppression of geniuses in academia and society at large.

In 1972

In 1972, I am the one who told the Congress that I claimed the Phallus symbol posthumously.

I Would Remind

I would remind the Democratic Party of the saying, "Still waters run deep."

What Are the Truths?

What are the truths that the Democratic Party are espousing?

The Standardization of Education

The standardization of education is a bad idea, because it produces educational clones, which is not conducive to individuality, creativity, or originality.

Sound Weapons

Sound weapons are a great idea. I never thought of that. You guys are becoming aliens. :) (Israel)

I Would Remind the Ass

I would remind the ass that they still owe me my Ph.D.s, so please give me my Ph.D.s.

Sir Lancelot

Sir Lancelot means: Sir lance a lot.

I Own Nothing

I own nothing, because everything is nothing.

Sir Galahad

Sir Galahad means: Sir the gal I had.

Montego Bay

Montego Bay means: Monte goes to the bay.

Tobago

Tobago means: To the bay I go.

Mayaro

Mayaro means: May I row?

Jamaica

Jamaica means: Jam maker.

Trinidad

Trinidad means Trinity in Spanish.

Does Everyone Know?

Does everyone know that their distant ancestors were ugly, and did their distant ancestors know that they were ugly?

Camelot

Camelot means: Came a lot.

Advising All Military Veterans

Advising all military veterans: Throw your full support to the Republican Party.

The Trinidadian Navigator

The Trinidadian navigator left Port of Spain for the new world and found the natives in the new world to be friendly.

Why Do Blacks?

Why do blacks shoot themselves in the foot?

What Most Americans

What most Americans do not know is that there are a great many Americans who envy America's power, wealth, and prestige, and who want to see America destroyed.

If the Republicans

If the Republicans plan to concentrate on winning reelection to the House and Senate, then that is fine by me.

Bullshitters

Scientists are bullshitters, and they don't even know that they are bullshitters.

A Genius with a D Average

I would advise the Republican Party that only a genius with a D or worse average can surpass President Bush, so find a genius with a D average to run for president in the next presidential election. :)

What Is Wrong?

What is wrong with having a short attention span? Some of the smartest people in the world have short attention spans. What most people do not know is that psychologists hate people who are smarter than them.

Attention Deficit Disorder

Attention deficit disorder is a Nazi's diagnosis.

People Should Be Aware

People should be aware that the struggle to free geniuses from oppression will probably go on forever.

Who Would Have Thought?

Who would have thought that the Democratic Party would have become a Nazi Party?

Why Do Children?

Why do children have to be disciplined in school, if they behave themselves outside of school?

A Nazi's Diagnosis

Attention deficit disorder is a Nazi's diagnosis that is specifically designed to eliminate people like me from academia and was based on research carried out on me when I attended Brooklyn College and City College in the 1970's. The diagnosis is designed to make sure that people like me are eliminated from American public schools, because that would weaken America, while making certain foreign countries stronger by treating the same classification of students differently. In other words, attention deficit disorder was designed to weaken America, while making certain other countries stronger.

Advising Black Americans

Advising black Americans for the second time, get out of the Democratic Party, because the Democratic Party is a Nazi Party.

A Nazi Party

Everyone who believes in democracy, get out of the Democratic Party, because the Democratic Party is a Nazi Party.

Attention U.S. Government

President Bush, Senator Bill Frist, and Congressman Dennis Hastert: The Democratic Party is a Nazi Party, because attention deficit disorder is a Nazi's diagnosis. You are free to handle this information anyway you wish. May the Source be with you!

Advising All Republicans

Advising all Republicans: Throw your full support to the Republican Party, because the Democratic Party is a Nazi Party.

Advising All Democrats

Advising all Democrats who believe in democracy: Throw your full support to the Republican Party, because the Democratic Party is a Nazi Party.

The President and the Congress

President Bush and Congress: If you ever need my support, please feel free to ask me for it. I hope you realize now why I was being suppressed all this time. May the Source be with you!

My Battle Scars

Mental illness and psoriasis are some of my battle scars, and I am very proud of my battle scars.

Political Polls

I would advise all Americans to stop trusting in political polls, because they are now all untrustworthy.

Your Own Political Judgments

I would advise all Americans to trust in their own political judgments, because all other political judgments are now unreliable.

All Electronic Measuring Devices

All electronic measuring devices are no longer reliable, because their results can now be manipulated from government or scientific research control rooms electronically, so that the people who are doing the measuring cannot know anymore if the results of their measurements are true or false.

Patients Can No Longer

Patients can no longer trust their medical tests results, because their medical tests results can now be manipulated from government or scientific research control rooms electronically.

Science and Technology

Science and technology are not the problem, but it is people who are the problem, because people are no damn good.

No Matter What Choices

No matter what choices people might make, people are still the problem, and the problem will never go away, so long as there are people alive. :)

Perhaps the Only Solution

Perhaps the only solution to the problems of humanity is to develop advanced technosynergic computers as soon as possible, because I don't think the solution is paradise on earth.

Attention Everyone

Electronic devices that you purchase in stores can now be equipped with video and audio devices that federal, state, and local governments can use to monitor what goes on in every household in America. Yes, folks, Big Brother now knows everything about us. So what are we going to do now? :)

Take for Granted

Everyone should take for granted that the federal, state, and local governments know everything that they need to know about us. Welcome to 1984! This is Uncle Sam wishing you welcome to the future!

Should Be Left Alone

Most children with short attention spans are really geniuses, and they should be left alone to explore the intellectual universe, because as their attention spans drift away from the classroom, they go on voyages of exploration into the intellectual cosmos, since their minds are exploring and creating new and original ideas as their minds wander throughout the intellectual cosmos.

Are Ignorant or Envious

People who hate people with short attention spans are either ignorant or envious of people with short attention spans, because most people with short attention spans are geniuses of the most powerful kind.

Obey Your Inward Monitors

Attention everyone: Obey your inward monitors.

Stand Its Ground

If the U.S. does not stand its ground in Iraq, where will it stand its ground? Don't forget that there are more than a billion Muslims in the world. The Vietnamese weren't more than a billion strong and scattered all over the damn world.

The War Dead

Someday, all the war dead will be reincarnated using advanced technosynergic computers.

Now America Knows

Now America knows what it is like to be a genius, because almost the whole world hates and envies America.

The Rainbow Party

Democrats who want to get out of the Democratic Party, but who do not want to join the Republican Party, should form a new political party. I would suggest the name: The Rainbow Party for the new political party.

Venom

People like to spit auditory, visual, tactile, ballistic, and other forms of venom at each other.

Venomism

Venomism is the philosophical doctrine that states that human beings like to engage in venomous activities of all kinds.

The U.S. Government

The U.S. Government should be notified of any child with a short attention span, because these children have to be protected from people who want to do harm to them.

Is Going to Win

The Republican Party is going to win for the long-term future, but it should never become arrogant, bigoted, or dogmatic. Please remain tolerant.

Stating That Too Many

Stating that too many Americans are dying in Iraq is not a solution to Muslim extremism. What is the Democratic Party's solution to Muslim extremism?

It Is Obvious

It is obvious that Muslim extremists are getting intelligence and technical support from certain advanced Western nations. Folks, we are at war with the world.

The Military Draft

The military draft should be placed on standby status.

If Everything Is Sacred

If everything is sacred, then the profane is also sacred, including the devil.

The Water Supply

Folks, the water supply in America is no longer safe to drink. Bottled water is also not safe to drink. Get your sources of water intake from juices and other indirect sources.

Space Vipers

Americans are now Space Vipers.

If When You Die

If when you die you will go straight to Christ, what will you do when you get there? After you have arrived, what will you do for the rest of eternity?

If I Remember Correctly

If I remember correctly, I believe that the Republicans asked me about eight years ago what they should do, and I told them to find a genius with a C average, and let him run for President of the United States of America. That person turned out to be President Bush.

Support President Bush

Space Vipers: Support President Bush.

Prepare to Defend America

Space Vipers: Prepare to defend America from all enemies, foreign and domestic.

This Is About

This is about all challenges to American hegemony of the world, the universe, and beyond.

Zeno's Stadium Paradox

Zeno's stadium paradox about half the time being equal to its double is false, because he was confusing distance with time. Distance and time are two separate issues.

Bill Cosby

Bill Cosby: I support you one hundred percent. You are right on target. Keep up the good work.

Condoleezza Rice

Condoleezza Rice: I wish there were ten million black women like you. I support you one hundred percent.

Privacy

Privacy is a myth, because not even God has any privacy.

Who

Who is programming who?

The Jews

The Jews experience religious persecution, yet they are strong and united.

People Who Criticize

People who criticize religious people should also criticize nonreligious people, because nonreligious people are assholes also.

Criticize Nonreligious People

People who criticize nonreligious people should also criticize religious people, because religious people are also assholes.

Yes, Folks

Yes, folks, we are all assholes, because, if we were to place our fingers in the back of our behinds, we will surely find our assholes.

There Could Be

Folks, there could be a chemical or chemicals that are added to potable water, juices, etc. that are normally harmless, but which when combined with certain medications that are prescribed by doctors can cause serious medical problems for the persons who are on those medications. Folks, the word "doctor" is a very dangerous word.

Warning!

Warning! The word "doctor" is a very dangerous word.

My Medical Information

Schizophrenia. Diabetes Diet Controlled. Psoriasis. Hemorrhoids. Chronic Constipation.

My Medications

Takes Risperidone 1 mg. twice daily. Takes prn: Clonazepam 0.5 mg. twice daily.

Liberals Around the World

Liberals around the world: Thanks for mistreating me, because I wouldn't have been able to accomplish what I did accomplish if it wasn't for your mistreatment. Now, I will return the favor by mistreating you.

You Still Have

President Bush: You still have my full support. May you choose the right course of action. May the Source be with you!

My Medications Interact

My medications interact with potable water, diet drinks, and skim milk.

All of the VA

All of the VA hospitals are staffed by Democrats.

Please Support

President Bush: Please support the Armed Forces, the disabled veterans, and please overhaul the VA, because the VA needs more Republicans, since somebody has to protect life.

Perhaps

Perhaps, the hierarchical structure of education cannot be changed, but the fairness doctrine in education should be replaced by the neofairness doctrine.

Neoliberal Arts

Neoliberal Arts should be given a prominent place in education at all levels of education.

I Fought the Good Fight

I fought the good fight, but now I have to surrender, because there are overwhelming forces arrayed against me.

Congress

Congress: I surrender for the second and last time. I hand over my battle sword to you.

Paralyzed Veterans

Paralyzed veterans, please study the cover of the United Spinal Association's "Country Keepsakes" calendar for 2005. Please study it carefully, because the word "support" on the cover is doublespeak for "kill." The artist who did the artwork, Ms. Laurie Korsgaden, is not your friend, and neither is the United Spinal Association.

Attention All Americans

Please stop trusting in every potable form of liquid. We cannot trust anything anymore. What is the country coming to?

A Nest of Space Vipers

Space Vipers, let us show the world what it is like to disturb a nest of Space Vipers.

Please Tell

President Bush: Please tell the VA to leave me alone.

The Blue Hen

Why is the Blue Hen a cock? The odds of that being due to chance are zero.

Keith N. Ferreira

The odds of Keith N. Ferreira being due to chance are zero.

Delaware

Delaware means: De la Warr, which means: Of the war.

Sabbath

Sabbath means: Stab bath.

To Keep the Sabbath Holy

To keep the Sabbath holy means: To keep the stab bath in the asshole.

Part Three—Uncle Sam

Their Fair Share

Congress: Disabled veterans want their fair share of the pork.

VAMC Wilmington, DE

VAMC Wilmington, DE: Stop messing with Old Glory.

Old Glory

Old Glory cannot save the world and each individual from present and future realities, because only the teachings of Old Glory can save the world and each individual from present and future realities.

Most of the World

Most of the world loves great entertainers, but not great teachers.

I Support You

President Bush: I support you one hundred percent.

The Teachings of Old Glory

Neoliberal arts is the teachings of Old Glory.

Any Plan

Any plan to pull out U.S. troops from Iraq should be kept secret, and the timetable for withdrawal from Iraq should be revealed to responsible Iraqi government officials only.

Constipation

Red seedless grapes from California can relieve the symptoms of constipation if they are eaten daily and in sufficient quantities. This result is based solely on experiments carried out by me on myself.

Aspirin

Aspirin taken in high doses daily can relieve the symptoms of hemorrhoids, and it can also act as a sleeping pill when taken in high doses. These results are based solely on experiments carried out by me on myself.

A Moisturizer Cream

I use a moisturizer cream on the most badly affected areas of my psoriasis.

A Snake

Do not trust doctors, because their symbol is a snake. Take only calculated risks with doctors.

I Would Rather Be

I would rather be Socrates unhappy than a pig happy any day.

Governor Arnold Schwarzenegger

Governor Arnold Schwarzenegger: You are doing a great job. You must have studied some Neoliberal Arts. Congratulations! You are now the real Terminator.

No One

No one can perceive me, and I cannot perceive anyone, because all that anyone can ever perceive are the characteristics of one's own mind.

All Doctors

All doctors are witch doctors.

The Tail

I do not strike at the tail, instead, I strike at the head.

Of All My Ideas

Of all my ideas, my favorite is dirt bombs.

I Support the Religious Right

I support the religious right even if it destroys me in the end.

Trinidad Is a Disaster Site

Trinidad is a disaster site, just like the Trinity site is a disaster site.

Holidays

Holidays mean: Days on which one honors the assholes.

A Holy Man

A holy man is a man who is an asshole.

The General Idea

I think people have gotten the general idea of what it means to be holy by now.

I Always Knew

I always knew that the Vatican is very wise, but that they are not telling the truth.

Rat or Snake

Perhaps the word "doctor" should be replaced with the word "rat" or "snake."

To Live for Tomorrow

To live for tomorrow is to help ensure that one will live in a future tomorrow. In a future tomorrow, we do not necessarily have to be the same as we are today.

I Am a Christian

I am a Christian, if there is a dollar sign on the cross. :)

Does Anyone Really Believe?

Does anyone really believe that nongeniuses can save the world without the help of geniuses?

The Almighty Dollar

The almighty dollar was crucified on the cross in order to save our souls. Let us give praise to the almighty dollar!

The Atomic Alphabet

Repeat after me: A for atom, B for bomb, etc. Now you know your atomic alphabet.

Profound Literature

Profound literature should be transparent, while shallow literature should be opaque.

Dollar Days

Dollar days are days on which we honor the dollars. American heroes are dollars, and we honor our American heroes on dollar days. We spend our dollar days in meditation upon and contemplation of the almighty dollars and giving praise to the almighty dollars.

Class Dismissed

Class dismissed. See you at graduation. :)

Old Glory
http://philophysics.com

Index

978-0-595-36585-2
0-595-36585-X